D0198247

Cool Limbo

Cool Limbo

Michael Montlack

The New York Quarterly Foundation, Inc.
New York, New York

NYQ Books™ is an imprint of The New York Quarterly Foundation, Inc.

The New York Quarterly Foundation, Inc.
P. O. Box 2015
Old Chelsea Station
New York, NY 10113

www.nyqbooks.org

First Edition

Set in New Baskerville

Layout by Raymond P. Hammond
Cover Design & Illustration by Justin Winslow | www.justinwinslow.com

Library of Congress Control Number: 2011921533

ISBN: 978-1-935520-40-5

ACKNOWLEDGMENTS

Many thanks are given to the editors of the following anthologies, magazines and journals that published poems included in this manuscript:

Pushcart Prize Nominee 2006: "Stein on Bishop"
Gertrude Contest Winner 2005 1st Place: "Stein on Bishop"
Gival Press Oscar Wilde Award Honorable Mention:
  2007: "My Twin Sister the Drag Queen"
  2009: "The Break Up"
  2010: "On Turning 40"

Anthology: *Flamboyant*: "My Father was a Jewish Mechanic"
Anthology: *Off the Rocks*: "At the Filling Station (after Bishop)"
Anthology: *Poetic Voices Without Borders 2*: "Black Book"

5 AM	"Bringing Straight Friends to a Gay Bar"
A&U: Art & Understanding	"Black Book"
	"The Mythology of Death"
Black Robert Journal	"Interior Design"
Bloom	"Running with the She-Wolf"
Chiron Review	"Worse Than Cassandra"
Cimarron Review	"Between Apartments"
	"Brothers and Sisters"
	"Conjugal Visit"
Columbia Poetry Review	"The Yellow Bathing Suit"
The Cortland Review	"Professor Julian's Legs"
The Cream City Review	"Liz Taylor in Levittown"
	"Stein on Bishop"
Danse Macabre	"Warren and Billy: Three Years…"
Ganymede	"Faux Finish"
	"The Slip"
Gay & Lesbian Review	"boy witch"
	"Cosmedics"
	"Fighting Fire"
Gertrude	"Cool Limbo"
	"Vanity Smurf"
Knockout	"Fire Island"

LambdaLiterary.org	"Gertrude, you had Alice...."
	"Peter Berlin"
The Ledge	"Michele, My Shell"
MiPOesias	"A *Golden Girls* Prayer"
	"If Hello Kitty Had a Mouth"
	"Uncle Mame"
Mary: A Literary Quarterly	"Girls, Girls, Girls"
Mudfish	"At Tamika's"
	"Under His Skin"
New York Native	"War Babies"
New York Quarterly	"Lilith: Pre Pre-Nups"
	"Lounge-adelic"
	"Uh, didn't you get the memo?"
Poet Lore	"On Castro"
RealPoetik	"And wouldn't you love to love her?"
	"Monday Night Mah Jongg at Marsha's"
	"Nobody's Glamorous All the Time"
Shampoo	"The Hummus Sexual"
Skidrow Penthouse	"Babysitting on Mescaline"
	"Botticelli Bombshell"
	"Cover Charge"
Swink (online)	"Self-Portrait as Boy and Grey Ghost"
Velvet Mafia	"At the Filling Station (after Bishop)"
	"House Beautiful"
	"The Oversized Corduroy Comforter"
Voices in Italian Americana	"Broken English"
Windy City Times	"Goal Weight"

Some of the poems in this manuscript have appeared in the following chapbooks:

Cover Charge (Winner of the 2007 Gertrude Chapbook Competition)
Girls, Girls, Girls (Pudding House, 2008)
The Slip (Poets Wear Prada, 2009)

> "And wouldn't you love to love her?"
> from "Rhiannon" by Stevie Nicks
> "Venus Doesn't Glitter When She Stands Next to You"
> from "Garbo" by Stevie Nicks

For my mother Claire,

my older sister Pam

and my twin sister Michele...

*the first of many
powerful, protective and inspiring women
in my life.*

Thanks to Raymond Hammond and Ted Jonathan of NYQ Books. Roxy Hoffman of Poets Wear Prada. My fellow editors at *Mudfish*. The talented Jeffrey Horvitz for the author photograph. Justin Winslow for translating my words into his lovely cover art. And my friends, colleagues, students and family for their continued interest and support.

Special thanks to those who provided me with writing residencies and/or grants: Marilyn Nelson of Soul Mountain Retreat, Lambda Literary Foundation, Ucross, *Tin House*, VCCA and Berkeley College. And to all the poets I studied with at New School and various workshops elsewhere: Marie Ponsot, D. A. Powell, Molly Peacock, Mark Bibbins, Elaine Equi, David Lehman, Liam Rector, Laurie Scheck, Richard Tayson, Mark Wunderlich, Henri Cole, Mark Doty, Eileen Myles, Carl Phillips, Brenda Shaughnessy, and Eloise Klein Healy.

Heartfelt thanks to Julia Markus, who was there with me in Italy when I wrote the first of these poems and who always believed in my work.

CONTENTS

II. BOYS, BOYS, BOYS

"...it's fine—really—maybe even a good thing—
a boy who's got some girl to him..."

"Bedecked"
—Victoria Redel (from *Swoon*)

Girls, Girls, Girls

Cool Limbo

A harem of skeletons, my mother might have hissed
had she seen them (or what was left of them)
brushing their layered hair toward feathery perfection,
preening like satiated lions on plastic lawn furniture—
too casual to sweat beneath the July sun,
too made-up to swim in the pool
where I bobbed quietly on semi-inflated water wings
and watched my sister babysit me.

They'd paraded single file through the open backyard gate
with six packs and lit cigarettes,
all ready in their bikini tops and bleached cut-offs
to claim their surprise inheritance:
an afternoon and evening at a parentless house.

Whenever one thought to look my way
to see if I hadn't drowned
(a favor for my stoned sister
dissolving into Zeppelin or Skynyrd),
I was reminded: I was the hitch,
an inheritance tax, an outsider, a boy
gazing into this secret society.

Most of them didn't care
(or even know) I was there.
They cared for nothing
like it was a job:

Flunked Di Blazzio's class again
but I don't fucken care…

Anson's already seein' someone.
That bitch from Homeroom. Who cares…

So my old lady's got breast cancer.
After all that bullshit she put me through?
Like I'm supposed to care?

These brittle beauties
my temporary guardians,
wingless but lofty in platforms,
drunk at their post, uncertain of their mission,
stuck somewhere between:
not hippies/not yuppies.
Ladies in waiting with truck-driver mouths
and illegal tattoos (they were only fifteen):
butterflies, unicorns, roses.
The Harley guys they'd met hitching to the beach
could get them up to my sister's room for quickies
but never made them blush.

I was fascinated by their utter indifference
to parents, the world, even me—
bobbing, silent, aimless.
Yet *their* aimlessness transcended
this realm where everything and everyone
was *stupid* or *sucked.*
The suburbs, Carter, Disco, guys…
They didn't want to be their mothers
or anyone's mother
and fuck teaching, nursing, learning steno.
They just wanted to hang out
in a cool limbo: this yard,
beautiful and unburdened
even by hunger.

If Hello Kitty Had a Mouth

Maybe she'd just meow.

Or maybe she'd still be mute after all.
Perhaps give us the silent treatment
out of sheer spite.

She could become a feline AIDS activist.
Or a foul-mouthed comic, Margaret Cho style.
I bet she could tell us where Osama is.
Maybe campaign for president
of her own fan club. Go on *Oprah*.
Turn down Charlie Rose.

She might suck cock. She might not.
She might just say that she does.

She could snack on live Smurfs.
Wash them down with dry martinis.
Then vomit just to see what it feels like.
Or she might simply prefer kibble.

But she'll certainly need major dental work.
A whole set of teeth. Though she might not find
a veterinarian willing to take on such a job.

She could pop pills, blow smoke rings,
whistle, yodel, sing opera, rap. Or play herself
in a made-for-television movie. Win an Emmy!
Or complain bitterly when she doesn't.

She'll definitely ask for a real name:
I mean, come on, Hello?

Then curse her creator
for silencing her all these years.

She might visit mall after mall
to spit at the rows of plastic merchandise
depicting her freakishly mouth-less face.
Show up in court to demand a piece of the action.
Then—hold a CNN press conference
to offer a public *Goodbye* to all those little girls
who worshipped her so long.

And sure, she might secretly want them
to beg her not to leave.
But she'll know she's done right
when they so cheerfully say nothing,
nothing at all.

Monday Night Mah Jongg at Marsha's

coffee-brewing coven
Formica fortress
the gals all ready
giddy on crystallized sugar
spearmint leaves
and pecan-ring goop

gliding round after round
bridge table corners:
reform temple sister
-hooded social

the rant a Long Island chant—
Harriet's eldest engaged,
Norma's youngest at Yale—
chopped with Chinese
hands, suits: *North South Crack Bam!*

mentholated fog
further yellowing
the yellowed ivory
tiles shifting like tarot

to spell out for their fellow
broom-less ladies
of broadloom and shag
future generations of success

each fortune conceived, conjured
in long house-coat hours
not spent noshing or wagering
mere change-purse bets

Girls, Girls, Girls

Pre-K
Sherri Doyle and Jody Goldfarb were the prettiest in class
(despite Sherri's perpetually chapped lips)
and the only girls who let me play house.
My parents boasted, "He's got not one, but *two* girlfriends."
They didn't know I did all the cooking and cleaning.

4th Grade (Summer)
Jackie Reeseman gave me my first part—
in her garage production of *Grease*—
because I was "tall, dark and handsome."
When I kissed her (in the carnival scene),
sporting her dad's leather jacket and a sad attempt at a pompadour,
no one could see I was acting.
I had a new role: the neighborhood Travolta.

6th Grade
Maria Lozarro was too cool to be anyone's friend
since she modeled for Macy's catalogs and had a pet monkey.
But at our Christmas party, she pelted
our teacher, Dr. Zarko, with a cupcake
for calling me *Miss* Montlack
and saying I was "chattering away like a regular yenta."
An Italian girl, she probably didn't know what *yenta* meant
but modeling in Manhattan, she was sure to know
plenty of stylists and hairdressers.

8th Grade
Melanie Parson was the wispy blonde
to whom I dedicated all my poems.
She had a boyfriend.
No one could see what I (or her boyfriend) saw in her.
When they broke up, I no longer saw what I had seen.
I liked Karen Winters now.
Karen had a boyfriend.

Senior Prom
Kim Cavallaro was "Class Eyes": I never knew what she saw.
We held hands walking the boardwalk
while everyone else grunted and rolled in the dunes.
Another Bud? I kept asking. *More champagne?*
She thought I was trying to get her drunk.
I was hoping she'd just get sick or pass out.

College (Winter Break)
When I finally lifted my head out of the books,
I could see there were no girls around, thank God.
Just women now.
And men.

"And wouldn't you love to love her?"
—Stevie Nicks

platforms
like a mare on thoroughbred legs:
some towering foal
still teetering
on a previous life's terrain

her rasp:
those boot soles
scraping sandy gravel,
lightly lapping
rain-softened leaves

shawls
lending shape
to a breezy ghostess
delighted by her own sheets,
how they billow

the pose
of white arms extended
as sheer capes unfold
sorrows, secrets, hiding places
for the invisible

an icon:
childless
fairy godmother
mothering
the fairy child

Liz Taylor in Levittown

You wore her perfume, kept score of her husbands,
even delighted in her weight gain
back in the 70's—when you too had put on a few,
then were inspired to lose it all
(like she always did).

I still wonder if her *Cleopatra*
had anything to do with that green eye shadow
we insisted you throw away.

Yet from the kitchen table (while doing algebra),
I too watched that night
as she was ushered forward like royalty
for her Channel 4 press conference:
violet eyes blinking, curt smile glimmering,
hair teased to a threshold bordering on self-mockery
yet commanding attention—and you gave it.
"Chuck it all—I'll never finish before your father gets home."
The rice could burn, your family could starve
      but "That damn dog had better shut his trap!"

Another bone…then Liz took the mic.
I didn't know who to look at:
this movie star under a fire of flash
highlighting that hair, those jewels, those eyes;
or you in your terrycloth housecoat and Kmart Keds knockoffs,
lighting a Kent III Ultra Light
to heighten the drama.

I rarely saw you focus on just one thing—
always rushing, even your crosswords were done (or nearly done)
with the spin cycle finishing and your soap opera starting.
Not to mention the phone (and "That *damn* dog!").

But you waited for words of wisdom now, eloquence, power
to enter your world, our world: there—
on the border of Levittown
and Liz delivered more than I could
when on the verge of tears (rage), she demanded
the nation to *Wake up! See what's happening?*
to not fear the dying, her friends.

She wanted research money, voices of support.
She wanted education
and I was getting just that:
a lesson that distracted me
from X and Y
and what it all might equal
for me—in the future, in this kitchen, on this island—
every day becoming more and more
a man.

And yet she seemed to be teaching you even more,
so evident by the way you inhaled deeper, nodding,
agreeing with her on a subject
you'd never discussed, probably never pondered
except during your trip to "Frisco" when I was 10:
"We saw the Golden Gate, Alcatraz and oh yes…
the gays—very colorful,"
punctuated with a whirl of eyes that said much more,
too much.

She was too gracious to name names
—those heartthrobs (Rock) and characters (Liberace)
disappearing without proper goodbyes.
Why? Why? You almost cried with her.

I did not
but I could not
though I **could** have a glimmer of hope
when Liz invited us—the world, America, moms like you—
to ask *Where would we be without these people*
we passively watch die?
These incredible people…who contribute so much?

A tenser tone, more unsettling glare:
I mean, for God's sake, where would Hollywood be?
Where would I be?
—so bitter she almost scoffed.

And as I watched the rice smoking behind you
and heard Dad's car pulling up the drive,
I knew exactly where I was—
as if for the first time—
I was there, just outside Levittown,
and surprisingly I was not alone
in that crowded kitchen
which suddenly seemed to be opening up
and opening up
at the beck and call
of one girlish but seriously angry voice
that somehow touched my mother
who'd once again be racing
to catch up with time.

At Tamika's

In the tight kitchenette, petite like her mother,
whose wide face was heavy with frown lines,
rice and beans simmered but never boiled
on the back burner 24/7—a beacon, the house's pulse.
She didn't drive or speak English.
Doorbells panicked her:
Girl Scout? Mailman?
Jehovah's Witness?
Or me—that Jewish boy
who rode the bus with Tamika, steered her away
from the heavy metal kids
and offered eighth-grade Spanish:
Hola, Señora Santos.
Donde esta Tamika?
She'd smile—a vacation for her frown.
Her dental work shoddy by Long Island standards,
she was ashamed,
the neighborhood's only Puerto Rican lady.
We'd sit on the living room's gold velvet sofas
and practice rolling my rrrrrrrs
while upstairs Tamika added more tears to her jeans,
rearranged the six silver studs lining her left ear,
powdered away her olive complexion.
Come on, Michael, she'd call before reaching the bottom step.
Let's bolt—in no rush but always desperate to leave
the screen door behind us
before her mother had the chance
to say *Adios.*

Running with the She-Wolf

Metal Bitch Barbara before her mirror
coated with hairspray and cigarette smog.
Denim Prophetess seeing much clearer
than I, her Prince Darling—poor kiss-less frog.

She powdered her cheeks, suburban gothic:
fully bedecked just to smoke in her yard.
Was this a duty as the town *hot chick*?
Her spikey galaxy: I the co-star.

Since everyone thought us the steamy pair,
no one intruded or bothered to ask.
I watched her each night layer make up and hair,
grasping the need for presentable masks.

My tough leather headbanger well hid the lace
only I glimpsed as she kept my straight face.

Babysitting on Mescaline

she saw seventeen
secondary senses:

Scale
Season
Satire
Suggestion

Sanity
Satiation
Self
Stigma

Source
Spawn
Situation
System

Suspicion
Safety
Style
Simile

Significance

sepia swirled
stereo
see-through
sarong-ed Sibyl
stroller-ing cul-de-sac sidewalks
seeking slant
seed
cusp

cigarettes

Stein on Bishop

One could not deny that for her, being was expressing and being in the motion of being, and that to be in any other state of being, or motion, was to be unnaturally expressing denial of one's natural being. Some said of her, when those some spoke of her rarely spoken-about life in motion, that it was her rarely spoken-about life and its motion that set the motion of her art and its being into its natural and necessary—so necessarily so—motion. Others, like her, said little of the rarely spoken and little spoken of motion of her life, saying more of the art itself, itself saying so much more, more than what any others could say or deny or deny saying. Some said and say and will say of her that she was necessarily in motion in her words and her movement through words struggling to express struggle through the motions of her life always always moving and expressing moving.

Some will say little of this motion.

Others will say nothing or something.

Though certainly all will be moved.

Moved by the motion that was her being, her expressing, her moving—the motion being what it was, what it is, what it will be to be moving and to move being.

And that being Bishop is all.

My Twin Sister the Drag Queen

relishes life
always double-dipping:
No, seriously, sawlsa has no fat.
The elastic waistband beneath
her carefully bloused blouse
ever permitting easy breaths
despite her chain-smoking.

She used to do hair. In the 80's
when most of her clients
wanted Taylor Dayne bangs—
even the guys. But left it
for high-end toilets and faucets.
Long Island's #1 saleswoman!
She does highlights on the side.

Referring to herself in third person,
she directs her daughter (adopted:
Lord knows I've enough stretch marks!)
around the pool's patio
strewn with platform sandals.
Help Mama pick up her things.
Before "the gals" drop by
for afternoon daiquiris.

Her hoop earrings often double
as bangles (even anklets once).
After two "daiqs," one'll go missing.
Kimmie, darling, come help Mama!
Hawk-eyed Kimmie's reward:
Spa Day at my sister's former salon.
Kimmie just turned five.

When the neighbor's Dobermans
snarl through the chain-link
as Kimmie hoop-sifts the garden,
my sister automatically growls back,
silencing them as she did bullies
who were dying to shout *faggot*
whenever she let me bead necklaces
with her and the other "gals" at recess.

Later I'd offer up my strands,
secure the clasps behind her neck:
purple and pink patterns
I'd counted out like rosaries. Though
my sister left no need for prayers.

Goal Weight

chunky Tamika: Mocha of the light dark skin darker
than the neighbors' suburber Gerber kids
—white-listed black, she fired back
punk, ramming spikey head, thick wrist-
banded with the army brats and alternative closet queers
head-setting in the halls songs shouts screams, snarly Mocha
of the dirty sneakers, meaty thighs   detention again
fussing so femme (*as if*) with her pink Mohawk
Mocha went, left   flew

now see her be so CBGB
weeknight headliner
torn fishnet, sloppy eyeliner—all girl (not girlie) band-
ed with the freaky, hippie, crusty
she finally screams aloud, douching front rows
plastic wand, plastic skirt
sprinkling this downtown lawn, un-landscaped
blades of tattooed arms hailing, flailing
drinking her water, holy or not
they thirst, they grow   cleansed
green in the white stage lights
of shining black   Mocha

Haight Street shoe-shoppers don't see her
—no showstopper—in the harsh glare
where on the corner clutching
purse: vintage lunchbox (Darth Vader)
she bums cigarettes, quarters
kissing passing friends—with cheek (cold sore)
Mocha so thin, so light, but leaving next Thursday night
rehab, government sponsored   *don't tell my parents*
the friends passing promise
stunned by her pressing bones, loose plastic skirt
that beat-up metal lunchbox
collecting strangers' coins
for nothing at all to swallow

On Castro

You might be stopped and commanded
at 3 am—to help sift the curbside debris
for the rhinestoned Mr. Potato Head earring
some breathless Chinese drag queen—Ida Ho—
dislodged during her demure attempt to re-bouf
her bouffant, sashaying home in platform thongs
from yet another benefit for dyslexic children
of Neo-Buddhist-Jew dykes on bikes.

This may be the same revolutionary corner
on which Harvey Milk started his business—
down the block from Moby Dick's and Jackhammers,
where sagging gray men won't surrender
their black leather hot pants, admiring from stools
glossy be-glittered kids aimed for clubs uphill
or in the Haight—those boyish girls and girlie boys
passing like a sequin storm as you squat and pan
—some drunken drafted gold digger.

But when you discover that sandy earring,
Ida'll be so grateful—her outfit again complete.
My hero, she'll sigh. *You saved him. Now
his partner won't be alone.* And neither will you
or anyone there on Castro—never quiet or closed
to any wandering freak or square, native or foreigner—
and always just a little more American
than America is willing to admit.

Michele, My Shell

Yeah, he's the smart one, she'll tell you.
But I make the money. WINK.
So who's really the smartest?
The smarter, I say.
Her shrug: Meet my twin brotha, Mr. Nitpick.

Then off to a story, starting with a
So I'm at electrolysis... or   *Back in AA...*
somehow never garnering winces,
even from strangers.

In high school, spying over a book's brim,
I'd study her on the patio (warm days) in the den (cold)
tilting wet heads to comb through knots
or scooping gook from friends' recovering pink eyes.
One of the cosmetology girls, she was all hair nails skin.
I was nerves, trying to make Dean's List
while avoiding her aggressive "cosmo" friends.

When the principal posted
MONTLACK: 1st Place—Math Olympics
on the bulletin board
she let everyone (who was willing) believe she won.
C'mon, she said. *It may be my only fifteen minutes.*
I mean, I'm hardly the next Vidal Sassoon.
But you're smart, you'll have more.

More.
More is More—her motto
applied to makeup, accessories, gel,
for a while, alcohol.
Well into the Steps, she came to San Francisco
to apologize: "undo past wrongs" (like stealing minutes?).

I was writing my thesis.
What, is that like a book or something?

We shared my futon—the closest we got all week
until double dipping her nachos in some taqueria's salsa,
she let loose the plan: *I'm leaving hair for good.*
I mean, in most salons, there's more coke than conditioner.
And that's not where I'm at, ya know?
Besides, too many mirrors. I can't stand staring at myself all day.

Why? I wondered.
The weight? (less alcohol/more dip)
Or just time? (more circles/more lines)

She was going into high-end bathroom design.
Commission. Company car. *And More.*
Can you believe it—company car?
Senior year she socked a jock (cracking three of her acrylics)
for calling my cream-colored Firebird *faggy*
but I had to learn about it from friends.

I'll send ya a new toilet seat. Deluxe, she called back to me,
boarding her flight home.
Cuz, no offense, your bathroom's a sty.

I never did see that seat.
Instead, her first bonus,
a check: $100.
Money you once "lost"
that I uh, "borrowed."
Another Step.
I didn't cash it, relishing her signature,
those hearts above the i's.

These days, I tell people:
If you're planning to add on, refurbish, redesign…
look up my sister Michele—My Shell—
she'll hook you up.
She can sell anyone anything.
A showerhead, bidet—
even a full-blown vanity
I myself can't afford
not to buy.

"Venus Doesn't Glitter When She Stands Next to You"

And she knows it.

So she keeps a mercurial distance, arranging and re-arranging

her crown of coreopsis before the powder room vanity—

where Mother Earth chain-smokes and chats

with a pock-marked cousin

(you know, the pasty one who always follows her around)—

a grand entrance planned for quasi-twilight

when (she knows) you'll slip away

to another soiree just getting started on the other side of town.

Where does she get the energy? Pluto asks.

Mars, already bored without you, issues a trademark barb:

I've heard she's a fiend: coke, meth, diet pills…

Nonsense, blurts tipsy Jupiter. *Jealous gossip amongst the lesser stars.*

It's like this all night.

With poor Venus in her polished rhinestones

vying to be their diamond center.

Botticelli Bombshell

A beauty fiend   pacified

    motionless

but for a few stray locks
eluding their loose ribbon

    golden tassels
fringing her sensuous
         not sexual
     pale skin
       too serene
      even to pimple.

Breeze sweeps across
bare nipples
long lashes
    without a fracture
      in her gaze:

the original   heroin chic.

    She's still
with us
      not necessarily
blonde or white
    nude or female—

a vacant face

staring from buses
        billboards
    magazines:

a sad beauty
looking lost
      but posed always
          always

  having nothing at all
    to say.

Christopher's Mother

Does not hang on to her beauty
as tightly as it hangs on to her.

As tightly as her husband hangs on to her.

China in the grubby hands
of a clumsy child.

Hours of decoupage. Better
than conversation with him.
Surface treatment either way.

In her sixties. Slender.
Psychedelic muumuu. Just for fun.
Though she was too cool
for psychedelics
back in the 60's.

Only at home in rentals.

In neighborhoods
where they can't afford to buy.

Invites her sons to visit.
Far better hostess
than mother.

Until: *Thank God for Christopher!*
Let's face it: my straight boys?
Rather *dull. I mean,*
BRING…A…BOOK!

Then: *Did I just say that?*
Oh well...
Potato salad?

Family recipe. Served
with more vodka tonics.
While her husband shows off
her latest project.
His grandparents' dining table.
Completely puka-shelled and shellacked.
But for a mahogany leg or two.

Between Apartments

Tamika came again last night.
Usually she wants nothing serious.
Maybe a poem
or some junior high memory
to rise up from me: for a tickle.

But last night she crashed
a dream not devoted to her.
Barging in, needle-kissed
at her inner elbow's crease.
(Should've known
if a high could be had *there,*
she'd find it.)

As when living, she was not ashamed,
just edgy with enthusiasm:
her *I'm baaack again* smile
like those when she'd pop up,
newly returned from another summer recess
at her sister's upstate (their parents' last-ditch attempts).
Or later: home from her punk band's garage tour,
wondering if I knew of any bartending jobs.

But last night, she wanted me
to help her move: cd-crammed milk crates,
crooked clothes rack, beer-stained mattress...
She tugged me, breathless.
It'll be one-two-three. Promise.
It's the perfect place. You'll see.

I just let her pull at what wasn't there,
the way one semester
I lent her money I didn't have,
figuring her not repaying might keep her
from asking again.

Remembering that last night,
I let her ask and ask, pull and pull,
hoping I could avoid being the one
to lend her   insight
as to where exactly she was now.
Or more imprecisely
where—all boxed up and ready to go—
she was not.

The Yellow Bathing Suit

I pick it up, wring it out (wonder when
my niece started wearing bikinis)
then hang it out with towels to dry.
No doubt I saved her from a scolding.

My sister scolds even me: *You're 36.
You're throwing your money away renting.*
I tell her I'll buy. When I meet someone.
Yes, everything…when you meet someone.

Oh, Uncle Mike…Uncle Mike?
I'm asked to abandon my book and the a.c.
for another game of Marco Polo.
I know with her parents making dinner,
she and the neighbor girls need supervision.
Or maybe she just wants to include me.

Once again, navel deep in warm water,
I am repeatedly calling out a man's name
and reaching for those slippery children
as they bob (*There! No, there!*) faintly
on a periphery.

Lilith: Pre Pre-Nups

Oh, how I'm sure they rollicked...That is,
once he finally got over me—and himself!
Always too intimidated by my toys (and my topping).
One day it's *God! I can't take her anymore!*
The next, bitching and moaning: *Please find her. I'm lonely.*
As if locating me was all it'd take to lure me back
from my new rent-stabilized East Village duplex? Right.
Seriously, she can have the *Better Homes and Gardens.*
I mean, it's not the things or even her that annoys me.
It's just the way she takes the brunt, like some
mopey virginal fag hag (sorry, but she did fall for a fruit)
always second string, ready to give testimony
in everyone else's drama. Sad. Sad. And sadder
as she ages, loses his attention, privately eyeing
surgeon's brochures (lifts, peels, rib removal).
Probably blames herself for the kids' troubles too
while he just lays around watching the grass grow,
eating Fig Newtons and conjuring up what wife # 3
will look like, not even considering which other
part of himself might be lost in the bargain.

Cosmedics

She met Charles on a blind date her first month in the East Village. And had him sized up after twenty minutes on her dingy sofa. Her warm hand in his cool pants: *Dude, what's the deal?*

When he cried, she patted his back, chomping tortilla chips. Then dragged him to his first bar—that night—outlining the necessary. Like how to give a safe BJ and differentiate between hags. The "Needy" being overweight and dateless with nothing better to do than live vicariously through... And the "Trendy" being too fab for straight bars: too threatening to women/too tempting for men to take seriously. She said, *The Trendy wears gay guys like jangling bracelets while the Needy are seatsavers/designated drivers.*

Gerri didn't drive, didn't even have a license. To ensure her status? Keep from crossing the line?

But we had to carry her home more and more often: *I love my gay friends—no, no, you don't understand. They sooo get me. Inside I am a gay man. I mean, since I was six, all my friends have been gay—all my friends...*

We finally saved enough to send her to rehab for her fifth "31st."

Just before "graduating," she called to say the program was *Fab, simply fab. It probably didn't take, but all in all I feel fab.* And when I offered to send some things—cigarettes, mascara, magazines—she just thanked me and said, *Baby doll, that's so sweet. But like I said, I'm fine. Seriously. I don't need a thing.*

War Babies

My friend Astrid says her parents back in Germany
still wear signs of the war.
They spread it on their bread: butter, jam
as thick as the slice itself.
They'll never get beyond those days, she says, *the poverty...*
And now slaves to luxury,
she waits for them to choke
on those fat servings
or for their hearts to stutter and stop
clogged with Nazi cholesterol,
all their childhood fears of hunger.

Even my own grandmother,
a solid woman of usually few words,
was moved to speak in her Yiddish/English
of The Days...
An immigrant Jew—hers was a different story.
They used to throw tomatoes, she'd say,
arthritic hand over pacemaker.
Can you imagine? Rotten tomatoes.
We were sitting on the sunporch
of her Miami Beach condo,
playing cards: some game
she learned as a child in Russia.
And here was no better.
'Dirty paranoid Jews!'
Ha! What meshuggenehs.
Claiming we came to horde America's wealth!
Who is paranoid now? she'd ask
and then throw down an ace
in the final moment, final round,
as if to spite the accusations,

not at all to win
my pot of jellybeans, broken pretzel sticks.
Grandpa always said
she was a woman who saved her aces.

Paranoia's one thing.
But suspicion is yet another.
I was six years old and silent,
awed, confused, terrified
by the strange contradiction:
her tan, wrinkled skin
against that pale, taut accent.
The suspicious, she whispered,
are the ones who survive.
And don't you ever forget that, Bubeleh.
Don't you ever, ever forget.

The words have remained
in my mind and on my skin
spread thick as butter
on Astrid's parents' bread.
I am no child of war, no escaping Jew,
but I have still been caught in the crossfire
of some new terror
exchanged between men.

My grandparents, Astrid's parents,
I'm sure they remember
those pink triangles
amidst the stars of gold
though they had different views
from either side
of the buzzing electrical fence.

Today I am the electric
tangle of barbed wire,
a threat to my own flesh:
tingling with the idea of touch
in a time when I can avoid
the possible consequence.

I can still hear the high school halls,
parties, locker rooms:
They all deserve to die, anyway.
Words as loaded as my adolescent silence,
as bloody as the juice of tomatoes
dripping down my grandmother's young face.
You know, I try, as I'm sure she did,
to parade proudly through the memories,
trying not to cower yet again
at the safe, gentle touch of my own lover's hand
all the while aware that the suspicious survive,
the suspicious survive,
yet somehow convinced
that this very awareness
makes a sacred, pulsing part of me
feel like it's already dead.

on the answering machine,
nearly unrecognizable
without the *friggens* and *fuckens.*
(Hearing her, no one could believe
that her house was immaculate.)

When she'd found out
my sister and I called her
Foul Mouth Josie
to distinguish her
from Josie Next Door
and PTA Josie,
she fingered the airspace
over my mother's set table:
"Listen, ya bastards,
I'll kill yas both."
Stoop affection
she'd used to win over
her husband.

My mother savored
her naughty friend,
borrowing but diluting
phrases: "Chuck you, buggers!"

—Dis here's Josie, Claire. I'm...

calling from Miami
there for the gathering
of personal items,
the scattering:
her eldest.

—I'm hangin in.

"Hang in dere, Claire. Hang in
dere," that summer my sister
went to prison.
No other Jewish mother
understood ours—their daughters
off to BU and Yale.

But Josie's slang, broken nose,
stoned son—positive
the year after I'd come out.
Had she ever thought
"This was supposed to be
your boy, Claire. Not
mine."   He loved women.
Caught it/bought it?
from the kind of whore
who had broken her nose
back in Catholic school.

—Oh, for God sakes, Claire.

Her voice not *fucken* foul,
just bare
like the shore where he was strewn
or his apartment
packed up.

—He lived like a bum. A bum.

Especially compared
to her own spotless house.

—But it's done. We're on our way home.

Where her boys were
never taught or allowed
to fear a cruel God.
Just Josie
and her harmless mouth.

Faux Finish

You spray-painted gold
that cardboard pyramid
for my niece's ice skating routine:
the tri-fold—bottomless.
No one'll see from the bleachers:
another example of your audacity
to build without foundations.

How darling, mothers would say,
wanting to rent your talent,
fringe it with tassels or taffeta
to match Sarah's leotard, Lyndsey's tights.
Long Island mothers feel they've spent wisely
when they hire gay.

My niece tossed the pyramid
like a ten-year-old Cleopatra
when she heard you'd gone.

Done with props and themes,
she skates team synchro now
while I avoid sideline mothers
looking for my "artist in residence."

Cinderella in Wonderland

Why ever would you wait for a prince to come?
Don't you know they come fast as they go?

Well, it's no worse than chasing rabbits—
I made him find me. Easy girls follow.

Now, no need to take a tone, Cindy.
I merely ask for your own good.

You certainly ask lots of questions, Alice.
Like some kind of Little Red Riding Hood.

Oh, but **she** was no wolf's dinner!
She needed no man to save her life.

I thought I was coming for tea today.
I thought we were going to play nice.

Well, at least wait for my friend Pippy.
The redhead I've been telling you about?

Why? So she can look down her freckles at (lil' ol' fashioned) me?
I've my step-sisters to put me down.

Oh, dear Cindy, I'm so sorry.
Really, we're only trying to help.

Help me leave my husband's castle?
Help me question my sense of self?

Of course! I've always been one for questions.
How else will we girls get ahead?

Sleeping Beauty was at peace sleeping.
Snow White—so pure when she was dead.

Are you **madder** than the Hatter?
Just wait until Pippy gets a load of this!

Oh, I bet Pippy doesn't even like boys.
I bet Pippy's never been kissed.

I've a mind to sic the Queen on you.
Now there's a lady who takes control.

I just don't see what the fuss is about.
So? I need a man to make me feel whole.

A *Golden Girls* **Prayer**

so that in old age I might...

ever coordinate my outfits
(complementing even those of roommates
and random houseguests passing through)

so that I might...
always reside with someone a full generation older
to alleviate the press of feeling next in line

so that I will...
first see the generosity in my slutty, bitchy and stupid friends
(or be seen as generous—if I am the slutty, bitchy or stupid friend)

so that I can...
resolve any life dilemma in a span of 30 minutes
minus commercials, credits
and theme song (*Thank you for being a...*)

so that I might...
just once say, "I'll be out on the lanai."

so that I could...
employ a gay house boy (even if it's just for one season)

so that I might...
embody Bea Arthur or at least live with someone
with balls like hers

so that I can...
call upon an unending supply of cheesecake
for every romantic crisis or bout of self-doubt

so that I will...
have someone to eat that cake with in the middle of the night
without being reminded of blood sugar
and skyrocketing cholesterol

so that I might...
click through my living room in heels too high for my age
never once slipping on the terra cotta tiles and breaking a hip

Nobody's Glamorous All the Time

My Aunt Pauline was a Jersey City stunner
and nearly everyone said she should've been
the Diana Ross of the Jewish Supremes
because she and her sisters—Sylvia and my mother,
all redheads: copper, carrot, crimson—
shimmied at cocktail parties in similar sequins and sheens.
And though only my mother could actually sing,
Pauline entered a catered event,
even in her less-crimson sixties,
like she was the new bride
or mitzvah itself.

All of her husbands died died died,
each creating space for the next
so that my Aunt Pauline always had
some romance or heartache
in her small beaded clutch,
too garish for funerals, too compact
for her new man's nitroglycerin.

After the third was gone,
she moved to Fort Lauderdale
to live with her daughter,
the lesbian, whose partner
had her own live-in mom.

Four women in a man-less house,
still my aunt curled her thinning hair
and thinner lashes
before leaving her room
for breakfast
or going to the oncologist
or therapist, who prepared her for another loss:

the left breast later reconstructed
so at 80 she could wear
those strapless sundresses everyone expected
upon her fabuliferous entrances.

Like the one she had planned to make
before meeting her maker,
who would undoubtedly be a man
or in the image of one
or two or three,

and up went my Aunt Pauline,
hemline hiked for paparazzi.

Boys, Boys, Boys

TRIPTYCH

I. Self-Portrait as Boy and Grey Ghost

A boy marching up the drive, calling *See?*
Another diseased reservoir pigeon limp in his hands.
See?   As if to say *Look at what I have seen.*
Not at who I am.

More pointer than hunter. Like his Weimaraner
leashed to the porch each afternoon,
too distracted by the shadows of moving birds
to be concerned with someone else's find.

The quiet of this dog. Not its lack of language.

How it'd been immediately hushed
to avoid upsetting neighbors, sleeping masters.
Willingness to be trained: affection.
Another way of saying *See?*   Or *I understand.*

Both the dog and boy—their shared knowledge:
where the grandmother stashes licorice
for blood-sugar emergencies: on the floor
beneath her bed, in an uncovered tin.

Their resistance to taking: a sentence never heard.
We understand.   The sentence tirelessly repeated.
More and more pigeons found.
Few revived, all of them offered.

Fighting Fire

I first felt it that afternoon in your family room
when you offered me your toy chest's newest claim—
the red plastic bullhorn, a miniature of your fireman father's,
a birthday gift for his only son:
Ten years old and nearly half my size!

Go on, take it! your voice projected,
the hollow horn's mouth aligned with your own
like a kiss I could see inside,
one that amplified some unspoken urgency,
a pre-adolescent emergency:
my own inner fire.

Really, take it, you said. *He can get me another.*

Were you casting off some hand-me-down
or trying to please me, your new pal?
I worried and wondered
if all my desires were as easily sensed.

I didn't want someone else's present.
What I wanted was that kiss.
I was just scared
someone might hear.
So I buried it one night in my backyard
and prayed for your father's forgiveness
then swore I'd never again take
a gift I was not ready to accept.

At the Filling Station (after Bishop)

I was there.
One of the saucy sons.
And later saucier
than they had wanted.

The bored, sweaty boy
in oil-permeated overalls,
arranging cans to say *Exxon, on, on...*

Only a woman of detail
(and boys like me)
could have noticed:
my mother's needlepoint.
And her begonia. I nursed it
when the guys were out on tows.
Though I knew it would die there.

It was something to do,
an instinct, habit. Like
my mother's needlepoint?
Better than the old carburetor
I was instructed to take apart and rebuild
when there were no lines
at the pump. Instead
I read paperbacks
(uninterested in my dad's
old comics lying about).
Or imitated (under my breath)
phrases seeping like fumes
from the head mechanic's lips.
Dis radiator's a real pissa.
A real cocksucka.

My father's Camel non-filters ever fixed
like an on/off switch for his face.
Mostly off. I waited
on the office wicker sofa
for an explosion *(Be careful
with that match!)*
every time he ducked
under a steaming open hood.
But it never came.

Maybe somebody does love us all.
At least loves enough to notice.

boy witch

for three Halloweens
your mother, beautiful enough
to halt your old man's remarks
with a simple eye roll,
would allow, even encourage it:
buying the green face paint,
sewing and then letting down
the hems each year herself—

had your plastic wand worked:
perhaps a daughter for your mother?
or a sister for you
instead of two older brothers.
maybe a potion to keep you
from outgrowing them,
some spell to stop them
from expecting tackle football.

but at seven there was no more
fabric to let out—and maybe
too little charm left in her eyes.
what a miserable cowboy you made.
an Indian would have been excuse
to paint your face again.

but no, that year your mother
revealed just how little power
she held in the world, and you
realized how little protection
you could offer her, even with
that shiny new dime-store magnum
your father put into your hand.

Vanity Smurf

Well, of course he stared at himself all day.
Everyone looked exactly alike—we're talking
a whole new dimension of clone here. Although
he was still by far the best looking of the village,
with a complexion even bluer than Smurfette's—
no doubt the result of some secret moisturizing routine,
perhaps a potion lifted from Gargamel's spell book.
Hey, a smurf's gotta do what a smurf's gotta do.

And expecting to be contented by workaday projects?
Gathering berries, thatching roofs, setting traps for Azrael—
all that drudgery and for what? To maintain some
god-awful strip of one-level mushrooms, like row houses,
a real estate fiasco (of mushroom-cloud proportions)
even the presence of ten Vanities couldn't appreciate.

His role was not entirely selfish, though—he
did introduce some much needed glamour and irony
(however unrecognized) in that saccharine world
always under attack and on the verge of being trampled,
where there was only a trollish Papa to be worshipped
but no Daddies, where males in Peter Berlin hip-huggers
were too busy skipping to strut, and where if a man
sought to eat you, it meant in that night's meager stew.

Yeah, if this is what you faced day in and day out,
wouldn't you cling to the familiarity of your mirror, too?

Broken English

In Frankie's house, there was no mention of

Tinkerbell or the tooth fairy—his parents

always busy (shedding their native tongue

or trying to pay rent). Though his father

once told him in broken English about

Pinocchio...Another Italian boy

who longed to be real. His mother started

leaving surprises beneath his pillow.

Articles about *fairies*. Who were dying

of AIDS. Frankie checks every night, even

at thirty-five. Expecting something on

the sheet. A message. A voiceless warning.

Clipped with care and folded. Like the coupons—

his mother, so poor, anxious, looked to save.

Professor Julian's Legs

Imagine them bared by shorts: stretched,
crossed on a sun porch's chaise overlooking
some lake at sunset—wine glass on knee, half emptied,
teetering with every deep breath or inflections
that stress ideas flowing easy and easier
upon each swallow, imperceptible degree of darkening.

Or on those cobbled roads, meadows treaded alone
in meditative stride or rushing off toward some goal
(espresso, bus, a book from that shop before it's closed)
or destinations unknown: the wrong lane, coincidental meeting,
a glimpsed scene or image for his poem. Or a man—
of meaning—with keen imagination, eye for thighs.

TRIPTYCH

II. Self-Portrait as a Young Man

Having never   touched
grandmother's tin of licorice.
Having never
tasted   *See?* or known
whether it was sweet
or bitter, like his salty sweat.
He wants to   *Understand?*

His Weimaraner dead years now,
having never   always yarded
or leashed.
Having never   tasted
the hunt, only the whiff
of diseased birds offered.   *See?*

Was it enough to understand?

No   repeated.   No
more willingness to be trained,
the young man forgoes dinners
for midnight sugar rushes.
His taking always balanced
with some resistance,
his own quiet sentence:

Indulgence is my craving.
As if to say   *Look. Look.*
I can almost see who I am.

Cover Charge

Some shadows fall where they will
but here darkness is part of the design
like the elevated dance floor, circular bars,
even this backroom, with exposed pipe, concrete walls.
I can tell by the neon lights angled downward,
revealing forearms, button-flies, shoes—
Just look at them!
>Penny loafers crossed casually,
>scuffed sneakers tapping to techno
>and boots—combat, cowboy, work, platform.
>Not to mention the sequin stilettos in the corner.
>I swear, they're at least a twelve.

Where would we be without our shoes?
What then would act as our faces
in this decapitating dark?
After all, wasn't it your worn-out Oxfords
that caught my eye, made me linger,
circling your awkward stance?

It's true—one look at those frayed laces and faded suede
and I decided you were the closest thing here
to what I wanted: an intellectual—subtle and sloppy,
>refined yet down to earth,
>the way many of my professors were.

Even now, as you pull me closer,
your hands clutching my hips
with strength I can't imagine any of my professors having,
I'm tempted to ask what you studied and where.

But I just trail my tongue
along the sandpapery stubble
and stop to kiss your Adam's apple,
wondering how, if you were to speak,
your voice might echo
in those great lecture halls, auditoriums.

It's scary, this vision I have:
you standing faceless in front of hundreds of students,
wearing nothing but shadows and these very shoes.
But when your hand reaches for my zipper
that picture fades and there are only the shadows,
laced with the sparkle of anonymous touches, tingles.

So this is what dark tastes like:
invisible but burstingly alive.

Peter Berlin

In a very real way…she's the purest art form.
I bet she said…just how many art lovers can one get to know?
"Greta" —Stevie Nicks

They call you Garbo of gay porn.
They call you *That Man,* meaning *The* Man.
They call you. They call you. And
they have called—decades now.

But there are no phones in the gutter
and the best beauty is mute.
Though some claim to hear you,
to claim you as ours.

Those hours posturing: patient tableau
fractured by a slow turn, directionless strut.
Destination: always *right here.*

Those same white hip-huggers and
you're never quite the same
canvas—on cobblestone, back-lit set
or a Fire Island boardwalk—
a briar your backdrop, there
where they wove your crown of thorns.

Vanity or generosity—Smut or art?
Just enough blur softens the image,
your blonde sweep.
First: lost and lonely Dutchboy.
Then: Penus Fly-trap.

But no one was *your* fantasy,
your leathered-up pin-up, *your* Peter Berlin.

Who nurses the nurse?
Sings the songstress to sleep?
Who, Peter? Who got *you* off?
Lured you down midnight streets?

Who left you standing on some corner
sparkling darkly in the dust
on the verge of verge,
wanting more and more hunger
without having had
even one little bite?

Bringing Straight Friends to a Gay Bar

is like showing photos of the trip to Africa
you will never be rich or brave enough to take.
Here are the gazelles, you could say, pointing
at the horny bar backs. *Yeah, they know me...*
Or introduce a particularly stunning giraffe:
the local drag queen too cheap or broke for club covers.

The colorless closet bore your straight friends once knew
grows hazy in the purple light as fashionable men
(whose names you forget) kiss you hello on the coat-check line.
*Yeah, they know me...*Your straight friends have never
kissed you hello. Notice how next visit they will try.

Better music, stronger drinks, your straight friends remark.
Tell them how last week you went shirtless and danced
on the tables. *Oh, is that why the bar backs winked at you?*
But when urged to do it for them now, you tell them
the first drunken display is sexy. The second: a faux pas.

Then explain how the bathrooms are unisex despite signage.
Suddenly feel beyond gender issues. Evolved. Sort of Swedish.
Or give the list of recent sightings: Nathan Lane, *Queer Eye* guys,
two senators, everyone's stylists. Watch them look for someone now.

And when they tire and leave embarrassingly early
to relieve sitters, you can page through one of those bar mags
and tell the drag queen (who doesn't hear you over the jukebox)
how your straight friends really love you, how they must
fully get you now, having finally glimpsed you here
in the light of this bar's dark. *Yeah, they know me...*

Then keep paging that mag until you find an ad for some new place,
one that will really show everyone just who it is you think you are.

Lounge-adelic

lavender lava lampery line lush lobbies
'luminating local long-winded loafers,
        lascivious lovers, lewd louses...
lanky limp limbs leaning loosely lopsided lavish leopard loveseats
lugubrious loners licking lightly lotioned lower lips,
        lukewarm lagers, liquors
luscious lime libation leftovers lining lacquered linoleum ledges
leather, lace, lamé, linen...
Levis, leotards, lapels, labels (Lagerfeld, Lauren, Laurent)
layering listless legions—
loquacious liberals, lipstick lesbians, literati,
        losers, ladykillers, lambs
lollygagging lawlessly, lingering laborless
letting lax language & limitless lazy laughter
lift
        lamentable losses, latent longings...
leavening lackadaisical libidos
luring lusty...leers, lays, lunges, liaisons
lassoing (if lucky) loaded Lords/Ladies leading 'legendary' lives
looming legitimate, large, leonine, luxurious
likely lapsing later
—lent less lenient light—
Lilliputian, ludicrous
lost, leaden
Lucite

Conjugal Visit

24 and 25—we could've been 16
the way we wrestled
there in the room
where you'd grown up, or tried:
shedding sneakers, watches, belts—
in the twin bed you once wet,
trying so hard to do it
the way lovers did on tv—
the actors like us, pretending.
Them: to love. Us: to know how.
All to Sting's sleepy beat
right there in Queens
above your parents' room,
vacant, thanks to your anniversary gift.
How proud they were
of their boy, travel agent,
sending them off to Pop's homeland.
PROUD TO BE ITALIAN—your dad's bumper sticker—
I'd read on the way in
before seeing the windows
I couldn't get over,
raised on Long Island *treatments*
not cast iron bars.
I'd never been over—part of the deal.
PROUD TO BE ITALIAN
Little did he know
his son, my stallion,
fumbled with my fly,
letting me gnaw
his neck between giggles,
whispering—even then
with everyone gone—
"Don't leave marks."

Black Book

At the end of the 80's,
he threw away his phone book;
everyone in it was dead.

Now strolling Christopher Street
to brunch and therapy,
he gazes into familiar doorwells,
remembering leaning figures, handlebar mustaches
curling, like fingers through denim belt loops:
those five o'clock shadows in the shadows.

He's 66, paunchy and gray
but they still wink at him from the grave:
cool invitations
to the piers, the truckyard,
back to their place.

Crossing the cobblestones,
he's still too stunned to be amazed
by all those faded one-nighters
lined up and waiting
for him to come.

The Mythology of Death

Hades, also known as Aides—
the "Unseen"—became invisible
when wearing his helmet, a gift
from the Cyclops.

Deaf to flattery, numb to sacrifice,
the underworld ruler was once moved
by the sad song of a beautiful and talented man
seeking his lost love.

Orpheus would later turn to men
after his wife died the second time.

Could even the god of darkness be that dark,
as to inflict the same grief twice, opening wider
the already infinitely gaping wound?
Greedy to sustain all his tenants,
his wealth of death, it seems yes.

Such power appears cowardly
armed with invisibility
against a weaker race
so dependent on sight,
(and to think—this gift,
for a god with everything,
had come from a creature
with just one eye.)

Do they—our lost lovers
and our lovers yet to be lost—
expect us to attempt similar
senseless journeys? To sing,
to beg, to offer our gifts
for yet one more chance
to lose them?

Helmet-less, we don
our only protection:
we already love men
and know how to turn to them
in the repetitious waves of grief.

My Father Was a Jewish Mechanic

In my twenties he told me things
he didn't tell my sisters.
Not because I was his only son.
But because I had what he called nerve
(for coming out during college).
Ya got a set a balls, kid, he'd say.
Bigger than your sister's even.

When he trucked my belongings
that second (or third?) time
from my boyfriend's place—
me crying most of the way—
he just said, *You boys need to shit
or get off the pot already.*
Then helped carry my boxes
into the house, where he told me,
Don't make yourself too comfortable.
The mechanic—he knew when things were unfixable.
Jamal and I were back together in a week.

But all those trips through the Village
had unboxed one of my father's own exes:
Marsha. Some girl from the bars
during his single days—part of his gang.
Driving down 15th, he looked this way and that.
Yeah, this here's the street, he mumbled.
The one he had circled for hours
after dropping her at the clinic that rainy day.
It was illegal then, he'd remind me.
Just like being gay was.
*And I thought the whole damn world
knew what we were up to.*
I sweated like a bastard 'til I picked her up.

He seemed amused by it all then,
remembering the panic, the bad boy
his own mother (and mine) never knew.
If he were alive today, he'd surely get a kick
to hear I wound up in a 15th Street studio
where I hole myself in on weekends
to write about these things,
peeking now and then through the curtains
as the cars blur by, the faces of all those drivers
resembling at least a little
that shaky young man on the slick road
who'd always manage to give me a ride.

TRIPTYCH

III. Portrait of the Selves Revived

The man lives in a city of apartments
too cramped for a Weimaraner,
perhaps even the memory of one.

But the skyscraper window ledges
temporarily shelve birds
See?   winged and dirty,
somehow toughened by pollutants.

The man can almost smell them
through his window's spotty glass.
Rank like the last breath of his dying dog?
No.   No, he never needed
to be that close   to hear
the language of the leashed,
the hushed.

Is it the stench of resistance
that he cannot remember
on that dog's tongue
as he stands before his window
too distracted by the movement
of these flightless birds?

Though he feels them
still limp   in his open hands
tirelessly offering their quiet,
their own language.
One he will never again speak
but will continue to understand.

House Beautiful

The mild one mixes fluorescent martinis
while his boyfriend guides the tours,
luring pairs of linen-clad guests
through lacquered halls, glossy rooms
visited by editors and on the verge:
their own spread.

Every now and then, he offers
a pause
before annotating: custom stained-glass doors
on some dead Dame's armoire,
now deemed perfect for DVDs.
Or some aside on costs, fine-line laws
to avoid when shipping
from third worlds.

His gestures—animated and precise
as a game-show model's—
alarm Baby, their drowsy French Bull
awaiting chase from her curl
on the lounge's silk throw.

No one leans on the treated walls
or rests a cocktail spent—
the coasters themselves (Venetian?)
worth framing.

Even the 70's spare room,
potentially *passé* anywhere,
seems *period* there.
How groovy, someone says,
the notion of a spare room
in Manhattan!

Then before pressing on,
the host bends to scoop
their quietly sauntering Baby,
collecting her in the cradle
of his long, gathering arms.

"Uh, didn't you get the memo?"

We're no longer doing your hair
or telling you what to wear,
arranging wildflower bouquets,
selecting colors for duvets,
treating your windows or your walls,
planning your galas and your balls.

We're like…busy.

Making our own lives
uber-fabulous.

I mean, why sing for supper
when the food tastes like shit?
Entertain yourselves, folks.
We boys have had it.

We're through making your soirees
more glamorous—or less pathetic—
filling lulls with witty remarks,
offering "unmatchable" aesthetics.

Michelangelo painted the chapel
that wouldn't marry him today.
But we're registering at Tiffany's,
arranging our own wildflower bouquets.

So take a course in Arts & Crafts,
buy a glue gun or sewing machine.
The support staff has been promoted!
Your court jester is now the Queen.

Fire Island

Our daring swimsuits confetti the shore:
neon plaids, paisley hotpants, leopard thongs,
mostly designer and a tad tight
—even the older guys.

We unpack Dean & DeLuca lunches, navigate rainbow kites,
recline in the shade of novels about ourselves,
perhaps peeling off those suits to let the sun worship us—
all to a soundtrack younger than our years.

At ease on these shores, we romp
unabashed, unburdened,
like sensitive creatures celebrating
the shedding
of suddenly unnecessary
shells.

The Hummus Sexual

wears sandals but no Birkenstocks,
knowing his wardrobe already
too closely resembles Peppermint Patty's.

His vintage shirts: garage-sale bargains
(not antique boutique rip-offs)—
he prefers a loose thread or barely discernable stain
to relieve his fear of being the first
to spoil a garment older than he is.

He diets not for a Fire Island physique
but to stay fit for his next trekking adventure:
some primarily lesbian tour company
all his girlfriends talked him into taking.
The only male on a dusty bus for three weeks
(though the gals assured him there'd be more)
he will have the best time.

He goes to therapy for self-exploration not crisis.

Considers giving up teaching for nursing
(or: social work for non-profit, some such).

He has no debts. He has no money.

He does not wear patchouli
and has not worn cologne
since being told by three lovers
(consecutive not simultaneous)
that his natural scent is like musk.

In no way opposed to group sex,
he will silently lecture with his eyes—
and departure—if anything unsafe occurs.
(Imagine his sandals squeaking
on the cummy tiles as he heads for the door.)

He is an activist not a politician.
A nudist not an exhibitionist.
Loves Radical Faeries but not enough
to be called *Tree* or *Prairie Dog*.

Dislikes admitting he dislikes Chelsea Boys
but understands: *They just have a case
of closet leftovers*—an urgent desire to fit in.

The first time he felt he didn't fit in
was in an all-male bar—so amazed
and disturbed by the artifice
of a completely womanless world.

He can be seen as *easy going* or *wishy washy*
but gets his aggression out in bed,
apologizing afterwards for having left marks
and blaming his sudden second erection
on his garlic-rich dinner.

He loves his mother.
And he loves his father.

He loves cock and balls
but is certain God is a woman.

He sends thank-you cards
for all occasions—in a sloppy hand—
and doesn't stop after being told:
No one sends thank-you cards anymore!

He does yoga but not regularly.
Plays guitar or hackey sack (whichever one, poorly).
Longs for San Francisco but lives elsewhere.
Looks like he owns a Lab or Retriever
but couldn't subject one to a cramped studio.
Has considered a commune and the Peace Corps.

He feels certain his sexuality is a gift
and tries every now and then
to express it in a poem (of sorts).
He'll read it to you after a few beers
and ask with eager delight
Whatcha think, whatcha think?
then buy the next round
for being such a good listener
though he knows you're already too drunk
to follow.

Under His Skin

at 15, his martini-mouth mother: *I know you're a queer*
Just make sure no one else finds out

16, Tacoma Grandma takes him in
never asking why he's come

17, art scholarship—New York

*

now 32, tattoos
      dragon, phoenix, Japanese clouds: all airborne
wrapping him like a shawl
biceps, shoulders, back
—nothing a dress shirt couldn't cover
should he ever trade
canvas for corporate
though they disappear
with a surprise naked
hug from behind

more artful
than Chinese characters (Life, Pride, Peace)
to him—Beauty, Delicacy
on a Nordic frame he wishes
less lumberjack, more ballet—
something that could be lifted
by Japanese winds

But permanence, he says
that's the real thing—they can't leave
then he says little more
slathering sunscreens
to help preserve that indigo shawl
as if even there—sand-speckled, sweating—in August Maui
he's warding off, like Grandma, a terrible chill
freezing fiery winged creatures in flesh
like howls
stifled in a jar

Worse Than Cassandra

"The curse of the artist,"

he said, "is the ability to envision
perfect beauty
in a blemished world
incapable of realizing it."

And the work of the artist?

"To try anyway."

Did he explain this
before or after the kiss?

The kiss of the artist:
inside his Bergdorf Christmas window
behind the mesh *In Progress* screen
that barely shielded us
from rush-hour shoppers.

We were progressing.
Two? Three weeks?
And already a work visit.

The crystal droplets
of the hot-air balloon chandeliers—
him leaning on a ladder
in paint-speckled overalls.
Cassandra herself
wouldn't have seen the blood
on those gold-and-sterling-leafed walls.

His glass bubble
squared, seamless, dustless:
agreeable mannequins
ever-accentuating each other
in postures merely suggesting
relation and motion.

Like that blonde standing solo
in sleek rowboat, collared
and wristed in chunky diamonds,
evening gown dry, stance undisturbed
by posterboard waves.

Fashionable refugee? Titanic survivor?
Whatever the catastrophe,
past or pending,
the mesh screen lifting
would only reveal the moment
or idea of elegance
even in chaos, uncharted seas.

The diorama excused from explanations.
His design portraying an excerpt
floating—if only

we could have maintained
that pose: two men kissing
in Bergdorf's window—
bold, sexy
and oblivious
(like the bejeweled blonde)
        to the Midwestern tourists

in town for Thanksgiving
and seasonal magic.

Should we—or he—have known
the ugly world never
would have held or showcased
us at our unreal best?

But the work of the artist
was "to try anyway,"
despite the curse, to create
an image of perfection
worthy of the occasion
but not so difficult
to disassemble.

Gertrude, you had Alice.
But I had him (so briefly) and now we don't even talk.

"Well, you could just call him. You could just call. You could. You could say something. Something about anything. About anything you might want to call him about. About him not calling. About wanting to call. About wanting him to call. About him calling you. You could say anything or something. Or even nothing. About you. Or him. Or you just wanting to call. Or you just wanting him. Yes, you could call about something, even nothing. Call about you just wanting him to call. About you just wanting nothing. Or wanting him. Wanting him to just want something. Want you. Or you to call. You could. You could say anything at all about him. About him not calling. About wanting him to call. Or him wanting something. Or nothing. Or wanting you to call. Or wanting you. Or something. Something of that nature. Or the nature of something. Of calling. Or not calling. Or wanting. Or not wanting. Or nature. The nature of wanting. Or wanting him. Wanting him to call. Or wanting to call him. Wanting him to want to call. To say something. Anything. Anything that might want saying. Before nothing more is not said. Before more nothing is said. Because nothing is more nothing than not saying something when something wants saying.

And that, well that's something."

The Slip

Is it possible
to have been tattooed
by someone's soul?

     Only with eyes closed
     can I trace outlines,
     a slight raise on my unmarked skin
     (even in creases: inner elbows,
     between fingers and toes).
     The designs always familiar
     but too abstract to identify.

I mean, can one be widowed
by the living?

     Carting the blank stone
     from days into dreams
     toward an open grave
     in my front and back yards,
     basement, bathtub.
     Ever eluded by the body,
     not the scent.

And if there is someone else one day,
will he sense this presence?

     The fine slip beneath
     my rumpled clothes.
     The railing I reach for
     even on shallow stairs.

Will you
be the mosquito netting
draping my honeymoon bed,
swaying almost imperceptibly in the dark
but allowing in breezes
that comb the hairs on my arms,
legs, chest?

The Break Up

But still, how scary it is—to find love
now when we have only ourselves
to blame for annihilating it.

We could have, Chris.
We could have.

Or maybe we could have been lucky enough
to celebrate Stonewall—only briefly—
before watching each other waste away
faster than civilized countries
could give our disease a name.

We could have been carted away to camps.
Patched in pink then forced to bucket feces
on the lowest ring of Germany's *Inferno*.

Once upon a time, we could have had little more
than occasional hours in rented rooms
as dark and vacant as our beard marriages.
Been trialed and sentenced like Oscar.
Or expected to condemn him
in polite dinner-party conversation.

The Oversized Corduroy Comforter

I bought
once I sensed you were going to leave
smells only like me. Sometimes like steam
when I sleep with it pressed against the radiator.
But mostly like me.

You often said my scent was stronger than yours.
Musky, you called it. *It gets me hard.*
(But my sister just says *B.O.*
whenever I crash on her sofa.)
You said everything about me was stronger.
That you hated how I'd likely move on
faster than you would.

My friend Paul's bed smells like pot
even when we haven't smoked.
Like his Medicinal-Marijuana-Activist boyfriend.
Especially at the end.

Paul and I have been sleeping together lately.
No strings. For company.
He calls himself a widow but says he knows he'll get by
when I hug him in the dark after we've come.

I'd feel foolish talking to him about you.
Because you're not dead. Or even sick.
Just gone.

Paul showers with lavender and lemon soaps
and burns Nag Champa nightly.
I think he's waiting for the pot smell to lift.
To know he's finally healed.

These days I like sleeping at his place.
Or at my sister's.
Because my bed just smells like me.
My 'musk.' Strong.
Reminding me that I'm not going anywhere.

Brothers and Sisters

Your older brother was stoned
during his bean-bag teens.
But at least would admit—
some twenty-odd years later—
that he had run away to Hawaii,
leaving you to fend off
Tacoma bullies by yourself
as your younger brother watched
through playground chain-link,
thinking but never saying
how much you deserved it
for ruining his reputation,
with your black nail polish and swagger,
pink-staining the family name
stitched into his Varsity jacket.

My older sister couldn't run
any farther than the length of our drive
in her platforms: bangled and baby-oiled
gladiator in the hedged den of our yard,
screaming over the Stones on her portable,
"Just try it, ya little fuckers!"
at boys on bikes who rode by looking for me
while my twin sister, barely beyond
doll houses, consulted me
with dog-earred Sears catalogs—
furniture and bedding crayon-circled
for her dream bachelorette pad
"fully equipped," she'd remind me,
with a spare bedroom decorated
with my particular taste in mind.

It's some time since we've ended, Chris.
But I still wish
I could've spared you somehow—
a sister.   Could have given you
some of that female love   so
you might've been strong enough
to believe a man could love you.

Interior Design (Boys, Boys, Boys)

The Basement: Daniel
foundation—early twenties
no longer dark or scary
a finished playroom: post-adolescent
glimpse of privacy

Roof-Top Viewing Deck: Roger
a telescope to locate him
though he rooted—there
behind me, preoccupied
with Venus or the wind chimes

The Bathroom: Two Quick Flushes
Scott at the vanity, clipping
snipping: *You're **not**
going to wear **that**?*
Or Eddie leaning over the toilet
hairy ass lifted, hairy toes jutting platforms:
Dunk my head, ya fucken bitch!

The Kitchen: Jamal
chatting chitty chat chat
eating my mother's matzah balls
watching games with dad
different team indifference

Master Bedroom: Chris
hugging sucking pipe-dreaming
less hugging, more sucking
jealous of Jamal's kitchen
a more-public *vertical* space

The Hallway: David
the long, narrow passage
that could've ended
in any room but...no-
where to sit and talk

The Family Room and Vegetable Garden: _____
mortgage: meaning   to get them
finally done
with summer shares
and rent slavery

Warren and Billy: Three Years into Fort Lauderdale

Warren's extended hand: *See, they do nice manicures...*

over there at the strip mall, where Billy buys chlorine

for the paisley-shaped pool seldom used—an unbroken blue

like the hurricane-free sky: *Don't let it fool ya.*

Even their feisty terrier has carved herself a nest

between their sleeping legs since they left New York.

And oh, some of these palms will never be the same:

Billy, so mannerly, in muddied khakis and clogs,

preacher's son, goatee whiter against black skin.

He introduces me to his flowers, even those dying.

The most spectacularly potted—housewarming gifts.

Always more and more guys moving in round here,

Warren says, *who knows, maybe in twenty years, Michael?*

And oh, Billy says, *such a marvelous school district too.*

Uncle Mame

—for Kimberly

As your grandma says, *Brush your teeth and eat your vegetables.*

But also eat sushi (brown not white rice)
and wild salmon galore—for your health **and** skin.
As for drugs and cigarettes...Need I?
Alcohol—only for happy occasions (to avoid dependency).
And drink water between rounds:
*Stagger cocktails so **you** won't stagger.*
Remember when I broke my ankle?
Don't tell your grandmother.

Wine for dinners and deep conversations.
You will have deep conversations, right?
Hopefully with a circle of international friends.
Learn a second, third, fourth language.
Travel outside the country. Inexpensively.
(Get to Barcelona.) And educate yourself always.
A Bachelor's can be tough but do-able (with the right major).
Then Master's is cake: all those people with the same passion.
Have passion. Lots.

Career always before love.
Achievements don't dissolve like relationships.
Long engagements—if you choose marriage.
And no children before 30.
Consider adoption: good kharma/no stretch marks.
Walk or swim half an hour daily
especially if you settle in the suburbs.
But you won't settle in the suburbs, will you?
Try a city with a country home or summer share,
preferably on the shore. Wear sunscreen.

When you're down—it's natural sometimes—
therapy before pills. (Remember Judy Garland.)
Cry until you're bored with it.
Turn to friends if boredom doesn't lift.
Like your grandpa says, *Your friends are a mirror.*
You chose them. Not that the grump has any.
Family is not your fault. Or accomplishment.
(Though you can take credit for me if you like.)

Never blame your parents. (Too *Mommie Dearest.*)
Society requires no certification for parenthood.
Hate them (or society) if you need. Don't blame.
Remember your grandparents, uncles, neighbors.
And the aunt who took you in. Pass it on.
Be what you wanted your parents to be.
(I try to be the uncle I always wanted.
Am I close to your version?)

Know every dark moment of your childhood—
even your mother's blackouts,
even her trading you for (permanent?) rehab—
is testimony to your strength, not God's cruelty.
Expect God's cruelty. Skate, write,
dance it away when it arrives.

Continue to save spiders and snails
from bratty neighbor boys' pestilence.
Take it up a notch. Befriend a queer
or overweight kid. Learn from their journeys.
Stick up for them when they can't.
Find your own style. Avoid trends.

Read. Observe nerds and unconventionals.
(Be a nerd or unconventional.)
They will go somewhere. Go with. At least visit.
(So few "cool" kids become "cool" adults.)

Love and be loved before having sex.
Then do what you like. You'll have learned the differences.
Enjoy your body. Protect it. No guilt
for wanting, seeking, attaining pleasure.
And don't tell your aunt I told you that.
No. Go ahead—tell her. Ignore all rules for women.
Remember most men are following rules too.
They're just less likely to know it.

Don't believe in Hell or any religion
that believes in Hell or its equivalent.
Study all religions. Cut and paste.
Find Nature, Art, Humanity, Charity.
Do yoga. Fear the God-fearing.
Drive across country. Expose yourself
to the unexposed: scary but crucial exposure.
Get involved in politics instead of complaining.
If you're not complaining, you're not thinking.
Think of your little sister!
Make a life-long love-pact with her.
Expect some disappointments. Don't hold grudges.
Tell her to "fuck off" in the moment
and look forward to hard but true reconciliation,
surely better than harmony laced with latent anger.

Always say what you think. Just at the right time.
Ask for what you want. Accept help with gratitude.
Work hard for what you need, harder

for what you desire (it won't feel like work).
Give advice only through example. And never upon request.
And don't take any from friends or—worse—family.

In fact, don't take mine.
Why are you even listening? **Are** you listening?
Good. Do what you want, what calls you.
Own but don't let it possess you.
Just please wear sunscreen while doing it.

On Turning 40

I remember those dinners with Warren and Billy.
In their Manhattan high-rise. At the table they'd bought
in Mexico. For their 20th. (The one they'd offer me
when they retired to Fort Lauderdale.)

But it was the console that always had my attention.
Six feet long and narrow. Mahogany. Like a casket.
Nearly covered with framed photos. All men.
In their twenties and thirties. Smiling. Cocktails raised.
Birthday candles. Marches on Washington.
Some 70's-style mustaches. Hairy pecs.
A few suits and ties. Leather chaps.
On Fire Island shores. Or was it P-town?
Couples. Singles. Some clutching dogs like babies.
And all of them looking back at me.
From across the dining room.

"You laugh like Joey," Warren would say.
After he had made me giggle (slurping his soup).
And Billy would nod emphatically.
Wiping his mouth before adding, "Yes, yes—
he does!" Then pointing at the gallery's
most 70's of the staches. "Beautiful Joseph…"

But they'd never say more.
Just that my smile was like Richard's.
My build—like Thomas. "No, Grant…No, Thomas."
"Thomas was much thinner," Warren would correct.
"Well, only that last year…" Billy mumbled.

And when I'd ask for details:
"It doesn't matter—We just remember the fun times."
"Only thing sadder than a sad old queen
is two sad old queens. Ha!"

Now I am older than their friends were.
When they died. Leaving all that space for me
at the Mexican table that has become mine.
But I still feel so young. Even when I see
the new lines and circles in the mirror.

Maybe each year is a candle on their cakes too.
I laugh like Beautiful Joseph as I blow them out.

About the Author

In addition to being the editor of the nonfiction anthology *My Diva: 65 Gay Men on the Women Who Inspire Them* (University of Wisconsin Press, 2009), which was nominated for a Lambda Literary Award, Michael Montlack is the author of three poetry chapbooks: *Cover Charge* (Winner of the 2007 Gertrude Chapbook Competition); *Girls, Girls, Girls* (Pudding House, 2008); and *The Slip* (Poets Wear Prada, 2009). His work has appeared in *The New York Quarterly, Cimarron Review, Court Green, Swink, 5 AM, Columbia Poetry Review, The Ledge, Poet Lore, Gay & Lesbian Review, MiPOesias,* and other journals. He has been awarded residencies at Soul Mountain Retreat (CT), Ucross (WY), Lambda Literary Foundation (CA) and VCCA (VA). He has also won a *Tin House* Poetry Scholarship and was a finalist for the Frank O'Hara Chapbook Award. He splits his time between San Francisco and New York City, where he acts as an Associate Editor for *Mudfish* and teaches for Berkeley College. He holds an MFA (New School), an MA (San Francisco State) and a BA (Hofstra University), all in Creative Writing.

About the Artist

An illustrator, graphic designer, and animator, Justin Winslow is also known for his cartoons that can be seen at mythfitscomic.blogspot.com. He is a graduate of the Maryland Institute College of Art and now resides in Brooklyn with his partner. For his online illustration portfolio, visit www.justinwinslow.com.

About the Photographer

Jeffrey Horvitz is a photographer living with his partner, kids, two dogs and cat in Portland, Oregon. He is currently working on his photo column called *Queer Aperture* in Portland, San Francisco, and Vancouver BC. One can view his work at www.jeffreyhorvitz.com.

About NYQ Books™

NYQ Books™ was established in 2009 as an imprint of The New York Quarterly Foundation, Inc. Its mission is to augment the *New York Quarterly* poetry magazine by providing an additional venue for poets already published in the magazine. A lifelong dream of NYQ's founding editor, William Packard, NYQ Books™ has been made possible by both growing foundation support and new technology that was not available during William Packard's lifetime. We are proud to present these books to you and hope that you will continue to support The New York Quarterly Foundation, Inc. and our poets and that you will enjoy these other titles from NYQ Books™:

Barbara Blatner	*The Still Position*
Amanda J. Bradley	*Hints and Allegations*
rd coleman	*beach tracks*
Joanna Crispi	*Soldier in the Grass*
Ira Joe Fisher	*Songs from an Earlier Century*
Sanford Fraser	*Tourist*
Tony Gloeggler	*The Last Lie*
Ted Jonathan	*Bones & Jokes*
Richard Kostelanetz	*Recircuits*
Iris Lee	*Urban Bird Life*
Kevin Pilkington	*In the Eyes of a Dog*
Jim Reese	*ghost on 3rd*
F. D. Reeve	*The Puzzle Master and Other Poems*
Jackie Sheeler	*Earthquake Came to Harlem*
Jayne Lyn Stahl	*Riding with Destiny*
Shelley Stenhouse	*Impunity*
Tim Suermondt	*Just Beautiful*
Douglas Treem	*Everything so Seriously*
Oren Wagner	*Voluptuous Gloom*
Joe Weil	*The Plumber's Apprentice*
Pui Ying Wong	*Yellow Plum Season*
Fred Yannantuono	*A Boilermaker for the Lady*
Grace Zabriskie	*Poems*

Please visit our website for these and other titles:

www.nyqbooks.org